Printed in the United States of America
First Printing, 2017
Teacher Appreciation Quotes and Gifts Publishing

44241443R00064

Made in the USA
Middletown, DE
04 May 2019